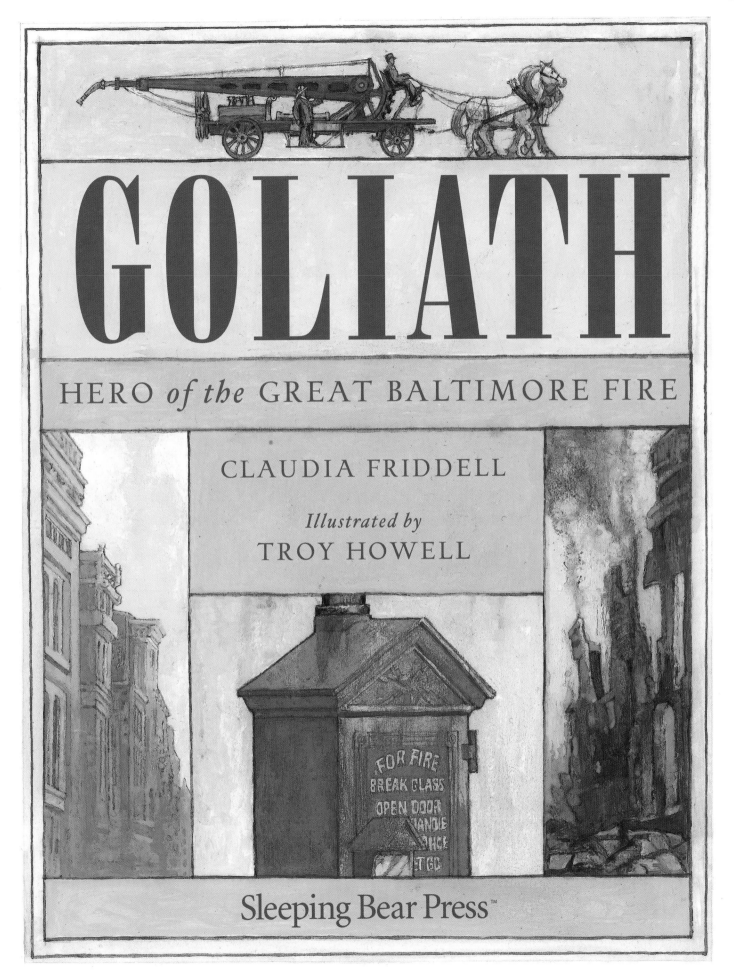

GOLIATH

HERO *of the* GREAT BALTIMORE FIRE

CLAUDIA FRIDDELL

Illustrated by
TROY HOWELL

FOR FIRE
BREAK GLASS
OPEN DOOR
HANDLE
ONCE
ET GO

Sleeping Bear Press™

Sleeping Bear Press gratefully acknowledges and thanks Melissa Marsh Heaver and Stephen G. Heaver from the Fire Museum of Maryland for reading and reviewing the manuscript and artwork.

Troy Howell wishes to acknowledge the following source materials as part of his research for his artwork: *The Great Baltimore Fire* (Peter B. Petersen) and *No Reason to Burn!* (George Welden).

Eugene Short with Goliath

(Postcard from collection of Gary Frederick)

Sleeping Bear Press™ • © 2010 Sleeping Bear Press • 315 East Eisenhower Parkway, Suite 200, Ann Arbor, MI 48108 • www.sleepingbearpress.com • Text Copyright © 2010 Claudia Friddell • Illustration Copyright © 2010 Troy Howell • All rights reserved. No part of this book may be reproduced in any manner without the express written consent of the publisher, except in the case of brief excerpts in critical reviews and articles. • Printed and bound in the USA. • 10 9 8 7 6 5 4 3 2 • Library of Congress Cataloging-in-Publication Data •Friddell, Claudia. • Goliath : hero of the great Baltimore fire • written by Claudia Friddell • illustrated by Troy Howell. • p. cm. • ISBN 978-1-58536-455-8 •1. Baltimore (Md.)–History–20th century–Juvenile literature. 2. Fires–Maryland–Baltimore–History–20th century–Juvenile literature. 3. Horses–Maryland–Baltimore–History–20th century–Juvenile literature. 4. Working animals–Maryland–Baltimore–History–20th century–Juvenile literature. 5. Baltimore (Md.). Fire Dept.–History–20th century–Juvenile literature. • I. Howell, Troy, ill. II. Title. • F189.B157F75 2010 • 975.2'6043–dc22 • 2009036941

*To Baltimore firefighters, past and present,
and my heros—Rip and Ann.*

*With special thanks to Gilman School, the Riepe family, Gary Frederick,
the staff at the Fire Museum of Maryland (especially Melissa Marsh Heaver),
and Esther, Cindy, Donna, Kathy, and Winn.*

— Claudia

To the children of heroic firefighters everywhere.

—Troy

On a cold February morning in 1904, a restless fire horse stomped and snorted in his Baltimore, Maryland stall.

While the other horses calmly munched hay along the firehouse walls, Goliath twitched from ear to tail.

"What's got a beast like you riled this mornin'?"
the hostler, Mark Hill, asked the dapple gray giant.

WHOOSH!!

The wind pushed Captain Kahl through the door of Engine
Company 15. "It's a nasty mornin' out there, Hill.
Don't expect to see many kids stoppin' by after
church to feed the horses."

Hill lifted Goliath's legs, one at a time, checking his feet
for a stray nail or piece of glass. His hands looked like a child's
next to Goliath's oversized horseshoes.

"Something's botherin' Goliath, Captain.
He can't seem to stand still this mornin'."

Standing still—that was something every fire horse was trained to do. They stood still in their narrow stalls day and night, ready and waiting for the sound of the fire alarm. They stood still while buildings collapsed around them, while intense heat blistered their skin, and while flames sent others running for safety. They stood still, unhitched from their rigs at the scene of a fire, waiting patiently to be returned to the firehouse.

Goliath had never had trouble standing still before. Just like his Percheron ancestors who carried knights into battle, Goliath was massive in size, mighty in strength, and steadfast in the face of danger. His company men called Goliath the ultimate fire horse.

Captain Kahl passed Goliath's stall on his way upstairs. "Last night was slow—he just needs to get out and stretch his legs. Take him for an exercise run this afternoon if things stay quiet," he called to Hill.

It appeared to be a quiet Sunday inside Engine Co. 15.
The horses were groomed, the brass was polished, the oiled
harnesses hung from the ceiling, and the company firefighters
were upstairs getting into full dress uniforms. Everything was
set for weekly inspection, except Goliath.

The one-ton stallion strained his massive chest against the
chain in front of his stall and slammed his twitching nostrils
into Hill's shoulder.

"You smell somethin' outside, don't ya?" Hill said as he looked
out the window.

Two boys ran down Lombard Street chasing after a runaway
cap. A woman's feathered hat flew off while her skirt wrapped
around her high-buttoned boots.

"Let's hope it's not a fire, big fella. That wind has a mind of its
own today."

Captain Kahl stopped at the top of the spiral stairway and called
down to Hill. "Only a few minutes until inspection. Do what
you can to calm Goliath—we don't want him spookin'
the other horses."

Hill had almost made it
to Goliath when…

BAM!!

Goliath slammed his foot into the back of his stall.

Before Hill could reach him, the house alarm sounded throughout the station. It rang out the numbers of the 854 Alarm Box on the John E. Hurst & Co. building on German Street.

"Turn out, men!" the captain shouted.

In a split second the entire company was running. Firemen slid down brass poles. The chains dropped in front of the stalls, and No. 15's fire horses rushed to their rigs and backed into position.

Goliath bolted to his lead position on the Hale Water Tower. The Spider dropped hanging harnesses from the ceiling onto the horses' backs. Buckle, snap! The horses were ready to go!

The captain hollered to his men, "It's only a thermostat alarm. Something's just overheated. I'll run ahead."

Hill shouted, "It's a fire, all right. Goliath smelled it."

In less than twenty seconds, the first teams raced the steam engine and hose wagon out the double doors and up Liberty Street.

Goliath bobbed his head impatiently as he waited for the second alarm to signal his rig. Goliath and his team were assigned the task of transporting the Hale Water Tower. It would have taken 60 men to pull this five-ton, 65-foot extension that blasted water into skyscraper windows.

"Hold your horses there, Goliath," chuckled the driver, Eugene Short, as he climbed onto the rig.

Just as Short strapped himself into his seat, the sound that Goliath craved rang through the station. The second alarm sent Goliath and his team flying over the stone streets.

In less than a minute, Short had parked the rig at the entrance of the Hurst Building, a six-story, brick warehouse stocked full of dry and cotton goods.

Smoke poured from the windows above as Short raced to free the horses from the rig and move them to safety. Goliath stood perfectly still next to the curb while Short unhitched his partners.

Just as he reached over to unhitch Goliath's trace …

An explosion of black smoke blew the roof off the Hurst Building, shattering all the windows! A piercing sound whistled from the smoking building as tongue-like flames lashed out of the entrance, scorching Goliath from neck to flank.

But despite his injuries, Goliath stood still, obediently waiting for a command.

Bricks began to fall. The building was going to collapse!

But the rig, blocked from moving forward, looked too long to turn around in the narrow street.

A crowd began to gather. Someone yelled, "They're trapped! They'll never make it out!"

Short snapped his reins and shouted to Goliath, the only horse still hitched to the rig, "Come on, champ! You can do it. Give it everything you've got!"

Goliath strained his massive chest and dragged the rig around, but the front scraped against a watering trough.

"It's too tight! They'll never make it!" someone shouted.

They inched forward, only to lodge the back of the rig into a telephone pole.

"They're stuck!"

EST.
1811

At the crack of Short's reins, Goliath lunged forward with all his strength. Without a second to spare, the rig finally broke free.

Just as they cleared the turn, the Hurst Building collapsed. Bricks rained down, burying a nearby steam engine and ladder truck.

Short, unaware of his own burns, buried his head in Goliath's mane. "You saved us, champ. If I hadn't been here myself, I never would have believed it."

He checked Goliath's blistered neck and flank. "You got the worst of it, that's sure." Goliath didn't flinch.

"Come on, big fella, you need some tending to, straightaway."

The thunderous explosion of the Hurst Building shook the entire city.
Within seconds, firebrands flew into the surrounding buildings.
Flames leapt from window to window and rooftop to rooftop,
spreading like an urban forest fire.

Frightened and confused, people poured out onto
Baltimore's streets, many getting in the way
of the firefighters.

As the flames continued to spread throughout the city, fire companies from Washington to New York rushed to Baltimore. Train cars delivered additional men and equipment.

Hundreds of policemen, soldiers, and citizens joined forces to battle the blazes.

S_s^sst.... BOOM!

BLAST! BOOM!

Demolition crews set off dynamite to block the spreading fire, but the explosions set new buildings ablaze instead. The windswept flames funneled through the narrow streets, alighting wooden buildings like matchsticks.

Firefighters battled late into the night under the glowing orange sky. The inferno continued into Monday morning. And the fickle winds shifted again and again.

It seemed that nothing could catch the fleeting flames.

It wasn't until late Monday afternoon when firefighters, fire rigs, and fireboats lined the Jones Falls stream to make a last stand. A wall of water blasts, pumped from the stream, finally halted the spread of the raging fire.

Engine Co. 15 continued to extinguish isolated fires among the ruins. Finally, two days after their missed inspection, the exhausted men returned to their station. They had served longer than any other company—55 straight hours! The men collapsed on their bunks, and the horses—all except one— settled in their stalls.

"How's Goliath? Is he gonna make it? Can they save him?"

Hill shook his head, "The doc says it's too soon to know. Burns that bad are tricky to heal. Any ordinary horse wouldn't have survived the explosion. But everyone knows there's nothing ordinary about Goliath!"

Over the next several months, children visited Engine Co. 15 hoping to see Goliath. Finally, six months after the great fire, Hill led Goliath, scarred but strong, back to the station house.

As Hill guided Goliath back into his stall, the company men gathered around him. Eugene Short smoothed Goliath's mane above his scarred neck. "Welcome home, champ."

Just as Hill reached up to remove his bridle, Goliath stomped and snorted, and his nostrils began to twitch…

GONG!

The house alarm rang through the station.
The captain shouted, "Turn out, men!"

… And once again, Goliath and Engine Co. 15 were off and running!

Afterward

It is guessed that a discarded cigar or cigarette dropped through a missing basement vault light and landed in a crate of cotton goods to start the Baltimore fire of 1904, one of the most destructive fires in our nation's history. One hundred forty acres and 2,500 businesses were destroyed. Miraculously, no lives were lost during the fire.

Only two years after the devastating fire, Baltimore citizens organized Jubilee Week to celebrate their beautifully rebuilt city. Their new hero, Goliath, draped with flowers and showered with cheers, led the parade honoring the 1,400 firefighters who battled the two-day fire.

Soon after the parade, a special act of Baltimore's City Council assured Goliath a home at Engine Co. 15 for the rest of his life in appreciation for his acts of heroism. Goliath led countless parades until he died at the age of 20. He was buried at Stoneleigh Villa in Towson, Maryland.

Fire Terms

Engine Company: A group of at least five firefighters assigned to a steam pumping engine or hose wagon.

Firebrands: Pieces of burning wood that are propelled by the force of an explosion.

Hostler: The firefighter who was responsible for the care of the company horses.

Lead Horse: Stationed on the far right-hand side of his team, the lead horse kept the rig out of the dangerous street curbs and gutters.

Percheron: One of four breeds of draft or work horses that were bred in Le Perche, France, and were ridden by knights in the Middle Ages. Because of their massive size, strength, endurance, and trainability, they made excellent fire horses.

Rig: A firefighting vehicle (also referred to as apparatus). Hose wagons, hook and ladders, steam engines, and water towers are all examples of fire rigs.

Spider: This metal rod held the harness above the horse's station in front of his rig. A spring tension was released and the harness and collar instantly dropped into place on the horse.

Team: A group of horses assigned to pulling a designated rig.

"Turn Out": This command signaled the routine a fire company followed in response to a fire alarm.

Having lived in several states, **Claudia Friddell** says that experiencing different regions of the country has given her inspiration for much of her writing. Wherever she has lived, she has worked with children; for the past twelve years Claudia has taught first grade boys. Of her work researching *Goliath*, she says, "It was a privilege to meet and interview firefighters and fire historians about the Baltimore Fire of 1904. I have gained an even greater respect for their loyalty to their profession and their pride in their history." Claudia and her husband have a son and daughter, as well as two miniature dachshunds named Camden Yards and Wrigley Field. They live in Baltimore, Maryland.

Troy Howell has had a prolific career as a children's book illustrator with numerous books to his credit, including *The Secret Garden*, *Favorite Medieval Tales*, and his own retelling of *The Ugly Duckling*. *Goliath* is his second book with Sleeping Bear Press; his first was *O is for Old Dominion: A Virginia Alphabet*. Also a fiction writer, Troy has a children's novel coming out in 2010. He lives in Fredericksburg, Virginia.